Penned in 3 weeks

Ayesha Bali

BookLeaf
Publishing

India | USA | UK

Presentation by *BookLeaf Publishing*

Web: www.bookleafpub.com

E-mail: info@bookleafpub.com

ISBN: 9789363310117

First edition 2024

I Found You

In every corner, under every stone,
I find it lurking, silent and prone.
"This isn't what I'm looking for," I sigh,
A trinket, a bauble, that catches the eye.

It glimmers at first with a promising sheen,
Promises of joy, unseen and serene.
Yet, as I hold it, the luster fades fast,
A symbol of a future that cannot last.

"This isn't what I'm looking for," I repeat,
With each encounter, my heart skips a beat.
Not for joy, but for the weariness within,
For this object mirrors a love that's wearing thin.

It's not just an item, but a metaphor clear,
Of a presence in my life that I once held dear.
A person, not perfect, who's worn me down,
Turned smiles into sighs, and upsides to down.

In every drawer, in every nook,
I find it there with the same old look.
"This isn't what I'm looking for," I mutter,
As my hopes, once again, begin to flutter.

"This isn't what I'm looking for," I confess,
To the mirror, to the stars, to the silent distress.
For the object I find, time and again,
Is an imperfect love, a bittersweet pain.

Obligation to Senselessness

My thoughts are a mosaic, composed of myriad
fragments,
Of chaos and order, a spectrum of views.
A labyrinth mind, where ideas ensue,
I am under no obligation to make sense to you.

Words spill like paint on a canvas so vast,
In strokes of emotion, the future and past.
Each verse a riddle, each line a clue,
I am under no obligation to make sense to you.

A symphony played on heartstrings so tight,
Melodies soar through day and night.
In dissonant chords or harmonies true,
I am under no obligation to make sense to you.

In dreams where the wild and the weirdness
collide,
I wander through wonder, with eyes open wide.
A world upside down, a skewed point of view,
I am under no obligation to make sense to you.

So let the stars fall, let the winds howl and hiss,
In my realm of reality, ignorance is bliss.
For in my universe, I am the rule,
I am under no obligation to make sense to you.

Ember Dreams and Silvered Tears

Bathed in your reflected glory,
I watch you paint the morning sky,
A fiery canvas, vibrant, bold,
While I fade to a mere sigh.

You burn with a passion I cannot reach,
Your warmth a distant, scorching embrace,
My love for you, a silent, lunar dream,
I yearn for your touch, an impossible trace.

You dance with the clouds, a playful king,
Your laughter echoing in the sunlit air,
While I, a lonely queen, in shadows cling,
My heart a silent, mournful prayer.

Bound by the cosmic tide,
Yet forever divided by the night,
You, the master of day, forever bright,
I, the mistress of the moonlit light.

I watch you chase the stars away,
Leaving me in the cold, vast unknown,
My tears a silent, silvery spray,
A love that can never be fully grown.
But still, I shine with borrowed light,
Reflecting your brilliance in the dark,
Hoping that in your radiant sight,
You'll see a love that leaves its mark.

In the silent hours, when you're gone,
I whisper your name to the stars above,
A yearning for a warmth that's never been,
A love that's unrequited, yet full of love.

But in the tapestry of stars,
Our story's woven, line by line,
Two celestial, distant scars,
Forever bound, forever thine.

Though we may never be as one,
My heart will forever be entwined with thine,
A moonlit love, forever unsung,
A love that burns even in the divine.

The Black Sheep

They nudge and prod, a chorus of white,
A mold for me, a path not quite right.
The black sheep, they scoff, where I stand alone,
But different isn't wrong, it's just my own.

Is following the flock the only way?
To blend and blur, to simply obey?
Their path well-worn, a comfort, I see,
But my own wild heart beats for what could be.

My fleece may stand out, a flag unfurled,
A different story in this grazing world.
I choose my way, a path less trod,
Unafraid of the whispers, following my own
god.

Seven Deadly Sins

In the depths of hell, where darkness reigns,
The Seven Deadly Sins writhe in chains.
Their twisted forms contorted in pain,
Forever cursed to suffer in shame.

Lust, the first sin, a seductive lure,
A craving for pleasure that cannot endure.
It leads the heart down a treacherous path,
Into the flames of eternal wrath.

Envy, the second, a green-eyed beast,
That covets what others have, and never cease.
It seeks to steal and hoard, to take and claim,
Till all that's left is a hollow name.

Greed, the third, a hunger insatiable,
A bottomless pit that's always unfillable.
It clings to wealth and status with a vice-like
grip,
Till all around it starts to slip.

Wrath, the fourth, a fury untamed,
A raging fire that cannot be tamed.
It lashes out with a burning hate,
Consuming all in its path, leaving only fate.
Sloth, the fifth, a lethargic haze,
A stagnant state that cannot be raised.
It feeds on idleness, and feeds on rest,
Till all that's left is a lifeless nest.

Gluttony, the sixth, a craving indulgent,
A feast of excess that's always abundant.
It gorges on food and drink, and all that's sweet,
Till it can no longer stand on its own two feet.

Pride, the last, the deadliest of all,
A self-obsessed ego that will never fall.
It sees itself as better than the rest,
Till it's too late to realize it's just a test.

These Seven Deadly Sins, so twisted and dark,
Will lead the soul to a fiery mark.
For when they take hold, they cannot be broken,
And the price of sin is always a token.

Monsters

You told me the monsters were never under my
bed,
That my fears were only in my head,
But little did I know, you were the real threat,
The monster lurking in my life, and I had not
seen it yet.

You told me to imagine a monster, so I did,
And to my surprise, it was myself that I hid,
But then you asked me why it was a monster,
And left me speechless, feeling like an impostor.

You made me believe I wasn't the monster,
That you were there to protect me and foster,
But as time passed by, I started to see,
The real monster wasn't inside of me.

You manipulated my heart, played with my
feelings,
Made me fall for you, with all of your dealings,
And I trusted you, without a second thought,
But you were only playing, the game you had
wrought.

Looking back now, I see the truth so clear,
That the monster was you, who I had held dear,
You twisted and turned, and played your game,
But all along, you were the one to blame.

Lost in The Quiet

In the hush of twilight's embrace, you whispered
faintly,
"Your smile is the brightest," you said too
quietly.
A murmur lost in the cacophony of the day,
My heart ached for words you would never say.
In the silence of my dreams, I'd repay,
For the things you said too quietly.

Beneath the stars' soft, listening glow, you
mumbled shyly,
"You're the one I look for," you said too quietly.
Words veiled in the shadows, never to be heard,
My heart burst with every unspoken word.
In the quietude, my hopes absurdly stirred,
By the things you said too quietly.

As dawn painted skies with hues of possibility,
"You mean the world to me," you said too
quietly.
In the solitude of morning, I stood all alone,
Wishing whispered words were etched in stone.
Yet, in my heart, love had grown,
From the things you said too quietly all alone.
Under the bleachers, sheltered from the rain,

A secret smile I hid, a whispered, "Isn't it
strange?"
"You looked pretty," you said too quietly,
A phrase lost in the downpour's roar, a plea.
My heart clung to the hope in his hushed decree,
I hate the things you said too quietly.

When the dusk wove curtains of the impending
night,
"You are my only love," you said too quietly.
In the twilight of their time, I finally understood,
His words were ghosts in the neighbourhood.
A silent love, never to be withstood,
Were the things you said too quietly.

Graduation gowns, a bittersweet and hopeful
day,
I held my breath, hoping you'd finally have
something to say.
"You mean the world to me," you said too
quietly,
A choked reply, a hand outstretched, a mumbled
plea,
My heart whispered back, "Will they ever be for
me?"
The things you said too quietly.

In the end, as stars witnessed their final scene,
"I loved you too," you said too quietly.

A confession unheard, a love unrequited,
All because,
You said it all too quietly.

The Sky's on Fire

Beneath the blazing canopy aloft,
Where azure turns to flames of softest gold,
The sky, a painter's final touch so bold,
Ignites the dusk, the stars yet seen so oft.

The horizon bleeds with crimson hue,
A tapestry of light that fades to night,
The sky on fire, a fleeting, burning sight,
As darkness comes, the flames bid day adieu.

Yet from the ashes of the twilight pyre,
The moon ascends, the night's cool, calming
bier,
The sky, once ablaze, now crystal clear,
Whispers peace, the fire's last desire.

Tangled Bones

In the hollows of the night, where shadows
dwell,
Lies a cryptic tale that the dark will tell.
Tangled bones beneath the moon's cold glare,
Whisper secrets in the chilling air.

Twisted limbs in a macabre dance,
A skeletal waltz, held in death's trance.
Each clack and clatter, a morbid tune,
Played by the wind, under a waning moon.

Entwined in earth's unforgiving hold,
Stories of the lost, untold and bold.
In the silence, they reach and yearn,
Bound forever, with nowhere to turn.

A world woven with threads of fright,
Bones interlocked, out of sight.
In the ground, they twist and groan,
A dark symphony of the unknown.

So heed the night's eerie, whispered call,
Of tangled bones that enthral.
For in the darkness, they might find,
The twisted remnants of mankind.

Hate You

Oh, how I abhor you,
For the way you bring forth a smile so true,
And how those sugary words from you doth
flow,
I resent how my heart starts to glow.

You make me feel vulnerable, feeble and frail,
And how you elicit that carefree laugh, so
unveiled,
I despise how you get under my skin,
And how you toy with my emotions with your
grin.

Your incessant annoyance, I cannot stand,
And how you never cease to flirt, so grand,

I detest you, oh so much,
But alas, I am but falling at your touch.

My heart, a slave to your every move,
I cannot stop the feelings, I cannot disprove,
I am succumbing to your charm and grace,
Oh, how I wish to flee from this embrace.

You have me entangled in a web,
A trap of emotions that I cannot help but dread,
I hate you, I hate you, this I know,
But I cannot seem to break free from this flow.

Your gaze upon me, a piercing dart,
Your voice, a symphony that plays in my heart,
I loathe how I have fallen so deep,
Please, oh please, help me to weep.

For the pain that comes with this adoration,
A love that is one-sided, a cruel affliction,
I hate you, I hate you, this I declare,
But deep within, I know the truth is rare.

For I cannot help but yearn for your touch,
To feel your embrace, oh how much,
I am but a fool, lost in this game,
A love that is one-sided, and brings me only
pain.

I hate you, I hate you, this I avow,
But my heart is no longer under my control now,
I am falling, and cannot break free,
Oh, how I wish you could see.

The heartbreak that comes with this love,
A pain that feels as if it comes from above,
I hate you, I hate you, this I know,
But my heart, it refuses to let you go.

It Sits at the Back of My Throat

A blush creeps up, a silent fight,
A tangled knot, unseen, but tight.
A warmth that burns, a word unsaid,
A hidden truth, a love instead.

Behind my lips, a secret kept,
A whispered hope, a feeling swept.
A fragile thing, with wings unfurled,
Aching to fly into the world.

The cage of fear, it holds me fast,
The risk of silence, how it casts
A shadow long, a doubt's decree,
"What if they don't feel the same for me?"

But love's a fire, a flickering spark,
And sometimes silence leaves its mark.
A chance unclaimed, a path unknown,
A seed unplanted, left alone.

So here I stand, a breath away,
To speak the truth, come what may.
For love's sweet song, it shouldn't hide,
I'll open up, and let it ride.

The Ballad of Seasons

Spring, she dances in on a breeze,
With blossoms in her hair and green on her
sleeves.
She paints the world with vibrant hues,
A touch of life, a fresh morning dew.

Summer strides in with a fiery gaze,
His days are long, his sunlight blazes.
He warms the earth with his golden touch,
A spirited laugh, a heat that's much.

Autumn arrives with a rustling sound,
Her cloak of leaves falling to the ground.
She whispers tales of the year that's been,
A mosaic of orange, red, and golden sheen.

Winter steps forth with a silent chill,
His frosty beard and strong, icy will.
He blankets the land with a soft, white coat,
A quiet strength in his snowy moat.

Monsoon, she weeps with a torrential cry,
Her tears replenish, as clouds fill the sky.
A symphony of droplets on every roof,
A cleansing dance, nature's own proof.

And then there's the season that's often unseen,
The one that rests between wake and dream.
It's the spirit of change, a transition's breath,
A time of rest, growth, life, and death.

Fading Echoes

When I'm alone, I often trace our past,
Of the laughter and whispers that didn't last.
Your face blurs, a fading watercolor,
I wish I could remember you better.

Letters and promises, once so bright,
Now lost echoes in the pale moonlight.
Your words slip away, like a forgotten letter,
I wish I could remember you better.

The places we loved, now empty and still,
Haunt me with memories I can't fulfill.
Your touch, a ghost, light as a feather,
I wish I could remember you better.

Seasons changed, and so did you,
From the warmth to a cold, distant hue.
Our bond frayed, a breaking tether,
I wish I could remember you better.

Miles stretched between us, a growing space,
Your smile, your voice, I can't replace.
You became a stranger, an unread letter,
I wish I could remember you better.

Time's cruel hand reshaped your heart,
Once open and close, now worlds apart.
You left, silent, no final setter,
I wish I could remember you better.

The dreams we shared, now just mine,
Fading slowly, with the passing time.
Your essence drifts away, a debt debtor,
I wish I could remember you better.

Your laughter, once a joyful tune,
Now a whisper, out of sync, out of tune.
You changed, a shift in life's barometer,
I wish I could remember you better.

The love we had, now a distant lore,
A tale of what was, but is no more.
You cut the ties, an emotional fetter,
I wish I could remember you better.

I reach for you, through the vast divide,
But you're a mirage, on the other side.
A memory fading, in the stormy weather,
I wish I could remember you better.

Our story closed, the final chapter done,
A setting sun, a love that's gone.
You're a shadow now, a mere silhouette,
I wish I could remember you better.

Fractured Trust

Beneath the moon's soft glow, we shared our
dreams,
Secrets wrapped in night's embracing seams.
A heart once open, now guarded,
Whispered promises, lost its feeling.

The stars that watched us, now seem to grieve,
For the trust that wove through the tales we'd
weave.
In the dawn's light, the truth unwinds,
Leaving trails of broken binds.

The echo of our love, once warm and bright,
Now a silent chill in the dead of night.
A soul once whole, now fractured by the strain,

A symphony reduced to a single, mournful
memory.

I stand, amidst life's relentless swirl,
A testament to a trust unfurled.
With heart's final plea,
I trusted you with everything.

Hand in Hand

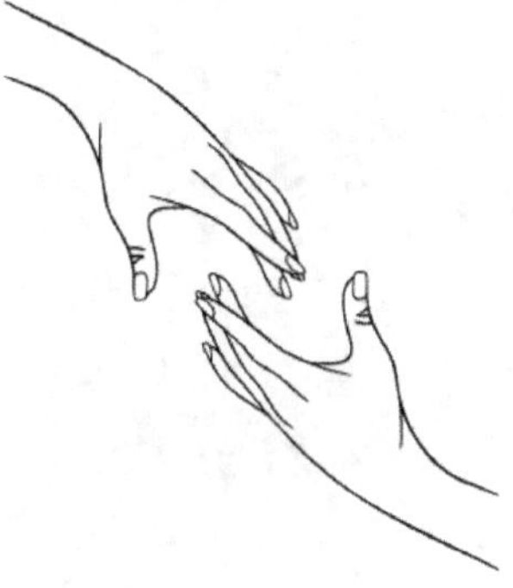

In hushed confessions, love unfolds,
A tale where yearning hearts are bold.
Through starlit skies and stories untold,
It's your hand, I crave to hold.

Soft as petals, your touch divine,
A symphony, our fingers entwine.
In the dance of shadows, secrets unfold,
It's your hand, I crave to hold.

Through the night, we roam,
In the sanctuary, we hoped to call our own.
Silent promises, like silver and gold,
It's your hand, I crave to hold.

In every heartbeat, a love untold,
A melody sweet, as the night grows old.
In the canvas of dreams, our love is scrolled,
It's your hand, I crave to hold.

Spirited Echoes

Have you ever wondered about the dance of
spirits unseen?
If ghosts truly existed, would they wander
through an eternal night, serene?

Perhaps they linger, seeking a hand to hold,
Yearning for connection in a world grown cold.
Do they find solace in the whispers of the
breeze,
Or are they trapped in memories, unable to
seize?

Would they dance in moonbeams, their essence
aglow,
Or fade into the mist, lost in the ebb and flow?
Could we bridge the gap between their realm
and ours,
With open hearts and empathetic powers?

Imagine the stories they could share,
Of ages past, of love and despair.
Would they guide us through the mysteries
untold,
Or simply watch as life unfolds?

In the quiet moments, when the world's asleep,
We contemplate the secrets they may keep.
For if ghosts were real, in their transcendental grace,
Perhaps they'd remind us of life's fleeting embrace.

So let us wonder, let us dream,
Of the unseen realms that may gleam.
For in the realm where spirits may roam,
There lies a beauty, a mystery to behold.

The Keeper of Your Scars

Was it supposed to be us?
In the quiet glow,
Hand in hand, hearts to trust,
But now, it's a mere shadow.

I see you with her, smiling,
A scene of my dreams,
Your laughter, bittersweet, beguiling,
A reality tearing at the seams.

We whispered secrets to the stars,
In a world that was only ours,
Now she's the keeper of your scars,
While I count the lonely hours.

Was it supposed to be us?
Dancing under the moon's gentle light,
Now I watch, silently, from the dust,
Love's lost echo, fading into night.

Keeping the Light On

In the heart of endless night,
When shadows creep and fears ignite,
I promise, here, to keep the light,
A beacon burning, ever bright.

Through storms that rage and thunder loud,
When doubt and darkness weave a shroud,
I stand, unyielding, true, and proud,
To guide you through the murky cloud.

When paths are lost and hope seems thin,
And weary souls seek the light within,
My lantern's glow will not grow dim,
A steadfast flame through thick and thin.

For every tear and silent cry,
For every time you question why,
I'll hold the torch and raise it high,
To light your way and never die.

In the heart of endless night,
When you need strength to carry on,
Look to the glow that shines so bright,
Know I am here, keeping the light on.

I Wish You Roses

I wish you roses, soft and red,
Their petals whisper love unspoken,
To grace the pillow by your head,
A fragrant dream, a gentle token.

Yet as I fall,
And darkness claims the room's embrace,
The roses' scent grows faintly cold,
A harbinger of darkened grace.

Their crimson hues turn nearly black,
Each thorn now sharp and dripping blood,
Once tender petals, now decayed,
Transform into a putrid flood.

Whispers morph to haunting cries,
As stems entwine around your bed,
Their grip constricts, suffocating,
Filling dreams with chilling dread.

I wish you roses, soft and red,
But hidden in their beauty's guise,
A curse entwined with every bloom,
A nightmare masked by sweet disguise.

Rustic Sonnets

In a house where whispers dwell,
A door with hinges, rusted cells,
Speaks of love, aged yet bold,
A tale of two hearts, never sold.

Its creaks are sonnets, old but gold,
Each groan a story, silently told,
Of years weathered, storms withstood,
A testament to love, misunderstood.

Though time has tarnished its vibrant sheen,
And wear has marked what once was keen,
The door still opens, a gentle plea,
A love that's old, but forever free.

For like the door, with its rusty sound,
Their love still strong, in it, they're bound,
Supporting each other, through thick and thin,
A love that's worn, but lives within.

So let the door creak, let it sway,
It's the music of love, in its own way,
A symphony of life, of shared sunsets,
Of love that's old, but never forgets.

It Whispers to Me

Beneath the sun, it slumbers, thin and frail,
But under the moon's pale gaze, it tells its tale.
A whisper in the silence, soft and low,
It speaks of things that only shadows know.

With every step, it stretches, grows, and bends,
A darkened twin, on whom your soul depends.
It holds the secrets you refuse to face,
The hidden fears that time cannot erase.

In daylight's realm, it mimics your facade,
But in the night, it worships darker gods.
It murmurs of the pain you've tucked away,
The dreams you've lost, the hopes that went
astray.

"Look closer," it implores without a voice,
"I am the echo of your inner choice.
The truths you hide, within me, they reside,
Your deepest self, from which you cannot hide."

It knows the fears we dare not name,
The whispered guilt, the hidden shame.
In moonlight's gleam, it dances free,
Unveiling truths we cannot see.

It whispers softly, tales untold,
Of broken hearts and souls grown cold.
A living ghost, a silent scream,
A fractured soul within a dream.

In shadows cast, our truths reside,
No place to run, no place to hide.
A constant companion, ever near,
Our shadow's whisper, fraught with fear.

Beyond Labels

You are not your grades,
Nor the titles that you bear,
You are not the money in your wallet,
Or the brand of clothes you wear.

You are not your hometown,
Or the job that pays your bills,
You are not the house you live in,
Or the number of your frills.

You are the dreams you chase,
And the fears you face at night,
You are the songs that lift your spirit,
And the battles you choose to fight.

You're the warmth in a hug,
And the kindness in your deeds,
You're the love you give to others,
And the way you meet their needs.

You're the books that shape your mind,
And the words that make you smile,
You're the memories you treasure,
And the roads that stretch for miles.

You are the laughter shared with friends,
And the tears you've bravely shown,
You are the lessons that you've learned,
And the courage you have grown.

You're made of endless wonder,
Of dreams yet to be fulfilled,
But it seems you often ponder,
On the things that time has stilled.

Remember you are more than labels,
More than limits falsely taught,
For you are wonderfully, truly,
All the things that you are not.

Unrequited Reverie

I sit and think about you,
With a longing in my chest.

Your laughter rings like music,
Your smile, a beacon's light,
Yet here I am in shadows,
Alone, each endless night.

I see you in my dreams, dear,
Where our hands entwine so tight,
But morning always shatters
These illusions of the night.

I whisper words of love to you,
That you will never hear,
They float upon the evening breeze,
Then vanish into air.

Your eyes are stars that guide me,
In a sky that's out of reach,
Your heart, a distant island,
On an unforgiving beach.

I cherish all our moments,
Though they're few and far between,

For in my heart you linger,
As a bittersweet routine.

You smile and speak so kindly,
But your gaze goes far away,
It's clear your heart's another's,
And beside them, there you'll stay.

I hide my love in silence,
A secret, sad and true,
For unrequited love is all
I'll ever have with you.

Shattered Time

At night,
When silence cloaks my fears,
I trace the scars you left behind,
With fingertips of tears.

Each memory a dagger,
Twisting deep within my soul,
The love we shared now shattered,
Has left me far from whole.

Your voice, a haunting echo,
That lingers in my mind,
A symphony of sorrow,
From a time we left behind.

I wander through the darkness,
Searching for a light,
But every step reminds me,
Of the love lost to the night.

Your laughter haunts my waking hours,
Your touch, a ghostly chill,
I can't escape the torment,
Of a heart that's broken still.

My dreams are torn and tattered,
By the weight of endless doubt,
So all I ask, in whispered breath,
Is give me time to bleed it out.

Fleeting Moments

Step back from the hustle,
And gaze upon your days.
Witness the threads of life weaving,
In such intricate, gentle ways.
The echoes of laughter and sorrow,
Entwined in a delicate dance,
The promise of tomorrow,
In every fleeting glance.

See your triumphs rise and fall,
And your dreams take flight then wane.
Every joy and each pitfall,
The moments of pleasure and pain.
The silent, starlit evenings,
And the mornings bright with hope,
The times your spirit's been tested,
And how you learned to cope.

Observe the chapters turning,
In the book of your own life,
Each page a testament burning,
Of victory and strife.
The whispered words of comfort,
And the storms that left you torn,
The friendships forged in fire,

And the new paths you've sworn.
Then marvel at the wonder,
This distance can reveal,
How all these small pieces,
Compose the life you feel.
The beauty in the chaos,
The strength in every scar,
How vast the soul's ocean,
How brilliant, and who you are.

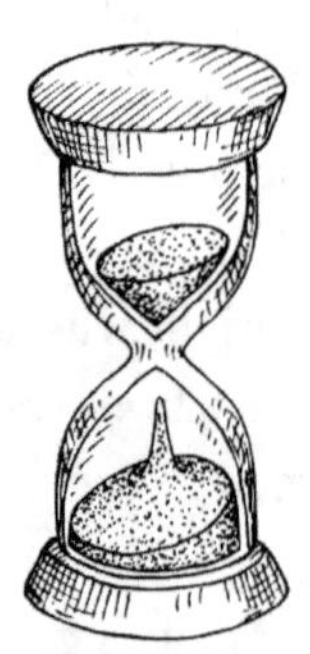

I Can't Say It Back

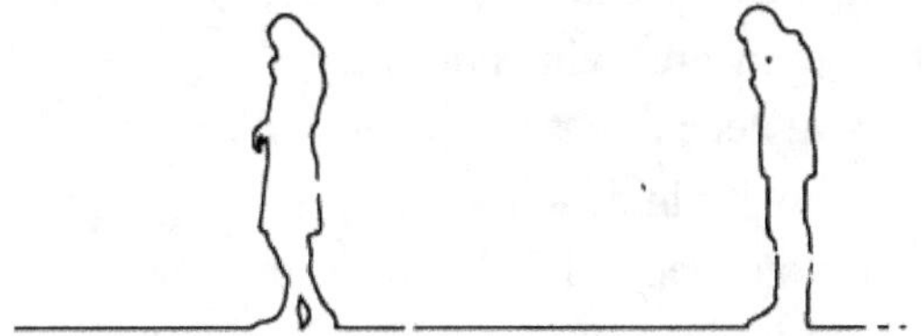

You said you needed to hear it,
Those three words from my heart,
But love isn't just in whispers,
It's been there from the start,
It echoed in the morning coffee,
I brewed just the way you like,
In the texts I sent to check on you,
When you worked late into the night,
It was in the extra blanket,
I tucked around you tight,
In the midnight drives we took,
When you just needed light,
It sang through the lullabies,
I hummed to calm your fears,
And in the tissues I handed you,
To dry your quiet tears,
It danced in the small surprises,
Like flowers left at your door,
In the times I picked up your favorite book,

From that little secondhand store,
It was packed in your lunches,
With notes hidden inside,
And in the way I stood beside you,
When you were trying not to cry,
So if you need to hear it spoken,
Just know it's in the air,
And if you ever feel the chill,
My love is always there.